My Favorite Machines

Planes

Colleen Ruck

A⁺

Smart Apple Media

Smart Apple Media
P.O. Box 3263, Mankato, MN 56002

An Appleseed Editions book

Planning and production by Discovery Books Limited
Designed by D.R ink
Edited by Colleen Ruck

Library of Congress Cataloging-in-Publication Data

Ruck, Colleen.
  Planes / by Colleen Ruck.
     p. cm. -- (My favorite machines)
  Includes index.
  ISBN 978-1-59920-677-6 (library binding)
  1. Airplanes--Juvenile literature. I. Title.
  TL547.R83 2012
  629.133'37--dc22
                              2011010385

Photograph acknowledgments
Getty Images: p. 21 (Brent Winebrenner/Lonely Planet Images); Library of Congress: p. 5; Nasa/Dryden Flight Research Center: pp. 17, 18 (Judson Brohmer/USAF), 19 (Tony Landis), 22 (Steve Lighthill), 23 (Steve Lighthill); Shutterstock: pp. 4 (Robert Sarosiek), 6 (Carlos E. Santa Maria), 7 (Monika Wisniewska), 8 (Ivan Cholakov/Gostock-dot-net), 9 (Perry Gerenday), 10 (Dejan Milinkovic), 11 (Ramon Berk), 12 (Margo Harrison), 13, 14 (S. Borisov), 15 (Ilja Masik), 16 (ncn18), 20 (Randal Sedler).

Cover photo: Shutterstock (John R. Smith).

Printed in the United States of America at Corporate Graphics
In North Mankato, Minnesota

DAD0502
52011

9 8 7 6 5 4 3 2 1

Contents

Planes New and Old

Planes carry us from place to place, high up in the sky. Modern planes can travel long distances.

This plane, called *Flyer*, made the first real flight in 1903. It flew for just 12 seconds, traveling about 120 feet (37 meters).

The Cockpit

The cockpit is at the front of a plane. This is where the controls are.

The person who flies the plane is called the pilot.

Propeller Planes

Propeller

This plane is powered by a **propeller**. An **engine** turns the propeller.

Some planes have more than one engine and propeller. This plane has two.

Jet Planes

Fighter planes and **airliners** are powered by **jet engines**.

Jet planes fly much faster than propeller planes.

Light Planes

Light planes carry just a few people. They can land in small airfields.

A microlight is a tiny plane.
It is not much bigger than a car.

Airliners

Airliners are big **passenger** planes. They can carry hundreds of **travelers** at a time.

Airliners can fly over long distances at high speed. They **soar** high above clouds and bad weather.

Cargo Planes

Cargo planes carry **goods** all over the world. They are wider than passenger planes so that extra-large loads can fit inside.

This plane is carrying a
space shuttle on its back.

Spy Planes

Spy planes carry cameras to watch **enemies** on the ground. They fly very high so they are hard to spot.

This spy plane does not have a pilot. It is controlled from the ground.

Seaplanes

Seaplanes can take off and land on water. They have floats instead of wheels.

This plane is called a flying boat.
Its body is shaped to float on
water, like a boat.

Rocket Planes

The fastest planes have rocket engines. Rockets are even more powerful than jet engines.

Rocket planes can fly very high.
Some have reached the edge
of space.

Glossary

airliner	An airplane that carries lots of people.
enemy	Someone who is against you and wants to harm you.
engine	The part of a plane where the power comes from to make it move.
fighter plane	A fast aircraft used to attack enemies.
goods	Things that are bought and sold.
jet engine	A powerful engine used mainly in aircraft.
jet plane	An airplane powered by one or more jet engines.
passenger	A person who is carried in a plane, car, bus or train.
propeller	Blades that turn and make an aircraft move.
soar	To rise high into the air.
space shuttle	An aircraft launched into space using rockets.
traveler	A person who goes (or travels) from one place to another.

Web sites

www.airplanesforkids.com
Learn more about different types of plane.

www.funpaperairplanes.com
Build your own flyers.

www.sciencekidsathome.com/science/flight.html
Find out how a plane takes off.

Index